women's rites

women's rites

Girlfriends' Rituals

CARMEN RENEE BERRY
AND TAMARA TRAEDER

**Andrews McMeel
Publishing**

Kansas City

Women's Rites: Girlfriends' Rituals copyright © 1998 by
Carmen Renee Berry and Tamara C. Traeder. All rights
reserved. Printed in Mexico. No part of this book may be
used or reproduced in any manner whatsoever without
written permission except in the case of reprints in the
context of reviews. For information, write Andrews
McMeel Publishing, an Andrews McMeel Universal
company, 4520 Main Street, Kansas City, Missouri 64111.

www.andrewsmcmeel.com
ISBN: 0-8362-5422-8
Photograph on page 11 © Lee Colquitt, Skipworth of
Memphis, TN.
Library of Congress Catalog Card Number: 97-81431
Book design by Susan Hood

The text of this book was previously published in *girl-friends* by Carmen Renee Berry and Tamara C. Traeder
(Wildcat Canyon Press, 1995).

One evening I came home from a
   quilting bee—
where twelve women, ages twenty-two to
   eighty-five,
had sat around a large quilting frame,
   working, chatting, and gossiping—
to find seven women gathered at Emma's
   kitchen table.
A party was under way. . . .

—SUE BENDER
PLAIN AND SIMPLE:
A Woman's Journey to
the Amish

Reasons to Rendezvous

Women have traditionally sought out other women, benefiting from the enjoyment of one another's company. Even when leisure time was nonexistent and home was the exclusive province of women's lives, women devised projects that would bring them together—quilting bees, canning vegetables, going to the marketplace to find food. While we may no longer need to sew our own blankets for warmth or can food in order to survive the

winter, women still need feminine companionship, and today's women have devised a number of activities around which to gather.

10 Over the ages, women have shared rituals
to honor every aspect of life. Some of these
rituals have been modified, expanded, and
incorporated into the fabric of life's most
cherished events: celebrating birthdays,

finding something old, blue, and new at a wedding, throwing a baby shower, and picking out flowers for a funeral. In the past, major life events were acknowledged in the community; marriages, births, funerals

were all part of the social order, acknowledging and marking the expected events in life. For good or for ill, life in our Western society is not so orderly, and a lot more goes on in women's lives today—other passages to mark, acknowledge, celebrate. We've collected ideas from women about their favorite girlfriend activities, and we've added some of our own favorites for celebrating friendships.

Birthdays

While we are officially celebrating our births, birthdays can draw our attention, sometimes against our will, to the aging process. Acknowledging that we've lived another year can be both joyful and painfully excruciating. Here are some of the ways the women we interviewed enhanced the traditional birthday celebration.

10   Have a professional photo taken with one or more of your special girlfriends to celebrate your birthdays. Rene and Carmen got all dolled up and had a photo shoot the year they both turned forty "as a milestone for each of us individually and for our friendship."

Construct a theme birthday party for yourself or a friend that celebrates being a woman. Nina found a poem that she shared with the women she invited to her party. Linda asked her friends to bring something

to read that contained some wisdom or feeling that her guest wanted to share with the birthday girl and the other guests.

18 If you are a mother of a daughter, give her the gift of your friends' wisdom. Margaret celebrated her daughter's twenty-first birthday by gathering Margaret's own friends together, those women she felt had something in terms of wisdom, direction or inspiration from their life experiences to share with her daughter. When her daughter is in

times of conflict or difficulty, she can replay the tape of the party and hear these women, ages forty to eighty, talk about the

hurdles they have overcome, the strengths and benefits they have gained, and what inspired them in difficult times. Margaret's daughter received the sum total of over a dozen women's accumulated life experience to take with her into adulthood.

Marriage

When a friend marries, throw a teacup party. Each woman invited brings a different teacup and saucer, reflecting her own taste, all wrapped up. After the gifts are unwrapped, they are used for a tea party. The bride keeps the teacups as a way of commemorating the women in her life. Each teacup is different and reflects the personality of the giver, and she is reminded of each of her friends as she uses the cups in the future.

22 Recognize your friends verbally at your own wedding. Kathleen told us about Elly, the first in her group of friends to get married, in which, "instead of going with the usual throwing-the-bouquet tradition, she made six separate beribboned bouquets

and tossed them to us from a balcony, one by one, with sweet words, during her wedding reception." When Jackie married, she wrote each of her closest friends, telling each what she especially valued about her.

When a new baby is coming, one group of
women we know gives the new mother a
handmade quilt in which each member

contributes a square.
What a lovely gift
for both mother and
child!

Welcome the new mother home with a much-appreciated gift. Elizabeth told us that she provides a welcome-home dinner for the mother and her family when they return home from the hospital. Or organize with several friends to supply dinners for the family for two weeks.

20 Make a time capsule for the new baby. Ask each of the expectant mother's friends to bring an item that personifies the age in

which the baby will be born. For an added twist, ask each friend to guess what she thinks the child will look like at age twenty-five, how tall he or she will be at that age, what line of work he or she will be pursuing, and so on. We heard of an African village tradition—when a new baby is on the way, the village gathers to speculate on why this child is being sent at this time, in this place: "What are we needing now that this child is sent to add among us?" The adults thus look at themselves and welcome the baby into that circle.

~

28 Have a speakerphone baby shower. Connie was expecting twin boys, and the night before her friends were to throw a big coed baby shower, she was rushed to the hospital to stop a premature delivery. At first all were discouraged by the thought of calling off the festivities, and then someone came up with the great idea of having two showers at the same time, with some of the friends joining Connie at the hospital and the others at the home site with her husband, Trevor. Connie and Trevor communicated with each other and friends via the speakerphone, with Connie first opening

one present and ooohing and aahhing and then Trevor opening another. So if you can't get the shower to the mother or the mother to the shower, or if you can't get all of the expectant couple's friends in the same location, a speakerphone baby shower will provide an experience no one will forget!

Writing
Connection

Keep those cards and letters coming! Most of us eagerly anticipate cards and photographs from friends who are far away. And it doesn't matter when we get them. Carolyn sends Easter cards, because that is when she finishes writing the cards she meant to send at Christmas.

32 Reconnect with a friend who has slipped away from regular contact by writing a letter to her, describing in detail one of your favorite memories of her.

Start your own creative writing workshop. Elise, Leslie, Sarah, and Michele met each week to pick a random topic, wrote together for a set period of time (such as an hour), and then shared what they had written. If you are interested in developing your creative side, this is a great way to do it. So far, Leslie has gone on to publish a book!

Holidays

Holidays are a great time to continue or begin a private joke. Kathleen confessed that she and her friend Maggie have sent a plastic poinsettia back and forth with their Christmas gifts each year for the last fifteen years.

In the midst of holiday craziness, Cheryl carves out a bit of time each year to get together with her friends for glasses of champagne. "As we sit talking and laughing, I think, 'This is great! I just love sitting here, and I'm so happy to be with these people.'" What better time to take a few moments to appreciate your friends?

On Independence Day, gather your friends together and have each woman declare herself independent of a specific fear or insecurity she has about herself.

Plan now for New Year's Eve 1999. Who better to include in your celebrations for the next millennium than your best girlfriends?

Traditions

Create a tradition. Find something that you do every year (or more) with the same friend or friends. Carey plans a river rafting trip every year for her women friends, which she calls "Amazons Down the River." Go to a local restaurant for high tea. One group of friends is crazy about basketball; they see high school, college, and professional games whenever they can.

42 Go to the spa together. Nobody but your girlfriend can appreciate the luxury of having a pedicure with you. Or create your own spa. Two office mates told us, "Whenever we have a chance, which is a couple of times a week, we give each other back massages. It

 relieves the stress, and it's a ritual we share together."

Plan an adventure. Rene told us about a group of single career women who take turns planning an adventure each month, known only to the woman who is planning

it. The adventure has to cost less than twenty dollars per person, and all the other women are told is what to wear. One month

it was hot-air ballooning. Borrowing from *Fried Green Tomatoes*, their secret cry is "Towanda!"

Go to the woods. Joanna and Kate love hiking and being out in the wilderness. "For both of us, the wilderness is a vital source of comfort and well-being, and our trips

always leave us feeling revitalized and at peace. We have been friends for so long that we are quite comfortable hiking along in companionable silence, although we also thoroughly

enjoy arguing over wildflower identification." Some friends are happier doing some urban hiking, otherwise known as shopping. Pick whatever refreshes you.

If you have children, encourage them to 49 talk about who their best friends are and why they like them so much. Start them off by telling what you appreciate most about one of your closest friends. Tape your story and send it to your friend. Not only will you be teaching your children to appreciate friendship, but your friend will always have a record of why you think she's won- derful.

Everyday Rituals

Some rituals may seem mundane on the surface, such as going shopping or sharing a cup of tea. But these womanly rites, whether grand or everyday, strengthen bonds of friendship and give us the courage and direction we need.

❧

52 Make lunch a special occasion. Rene and her friend use their lunchtime as a regular friendship ritual. She said, "We often want to talk without a lot of distraction or interruption at work, so we opt for an alfresco lunch in our favorite park, sitting on a bench or blanket in the sunshine. To spend a few moments with my dear friend and with nature can be refreshing to the mind and spirit."

Have a cup of java. Women used to take a break by sharing coffee over a kitchen table. Some still do, but many may be more likely to go to the local coffee shop. As Penny explained, "Sometimes, after a particularly trying day, we'll treat ourselves to a wonderful cup of coffee or cappuccino at our favorite little nook and enjoy the civility of it all."

54 Create a "wall of friends" in your home, with pictures of as many of your friends as you can find, in frames to match their personalities.

Organize a female film fest for an evening or Sunday afternoon at your home. We recommend *Strangers in Good Company*, *Fried Green Tomatoes*, *Julia*, *Postcards from the Edge*, *Thelma and Louise*, *The Color Purple*, *The Women*, *Boys on the Side*, and *Hannah and Her Sisters*. These are great movies about the strengths and weaknesses of women and the intricacies of their relationships, and they are sure to spawn a lot of discussion.

Just Between Us

Sometimes we rely on our girlfriends to help us grow. We might need to become more assertive, more honest about our feelings, or more confident in our decisions. Here are a few girlfriend rituals that women have used to strengthen not only their relationships but also their own personal growth.

58 Assert yourself! Claudette and her friend found themselves often apologizing to each other, as well as to others in their lives, even when circumstances didn't warrant it. To remedy the habit, for six weeks she and her friend each put a quarter in a jar every time either one of them said "sorry." They shared a dinner celebrating their newly found self-esteem by using the accumulated money to pay for the meal.

Celebrate a friend's new beginning (or an ending) with a spiritual housecleaning. Helen told us about a ritual her group of

friends enjoys whenever one of them moves into a new home or ends a relationship. "First, we meet at the house, in a serious mood initially, and burn sage. Then we go through the rooms of the house with lighted candles. Drawing from a Jewish tradition, we bring salt to sprinkle through the house to purify it. It starts out seriously—sometimes there are tears as an ending is mourned—but by the end we're a raucous group, opening the closets and throwing salt in. It's so much fun!"

Include your friends in your recovery. Nina, who was facing the truth of her own child abuse, composed a ritual to acknowledge that the image of her father she held as a child had died and been replaced by the truth. "I asked two of my friends to come and witness me burning items that symbolized my relationship with my father. As the items burned in the fireplace, I read the eulogy of the relationship between my father and me. One friend brought candles, and the other brought incense. It was a big step for me to ask them to support me and to let them give me what I had requested. It was very symbolic to me."

62 Enjoy being girls again. Get your friends together for a "big girl" slumber party. Or take them to the beach to build a huge sand castle. It's never too late to enjoy girlhood. Stop worrying what people will think!

Discussion Groups

~

Anne Morrow Lindbergh observed in the midseventies in her book *Gift from the Sea:* "The best 'growing ground' for women . . . may be in the widespread mushrooming of women's groups of all types and sizes. Women are talking to each other, not simply in private in the kitchen, in the nursery, or over the back fence, as they have done through the ages, but in public groups. They are airing

their problems, discovering themselves, and comparing their experiences."* Discussion groups come in many sizes and formats. All that is required is two or more women. Here are some of the ideas we've collected:

*Anne Morrow Lindbergh, *Gift from the Sea* (New York: Random House, 1975), 137.

Start a breakfast club. We heard of a group of women living in a small town who go to the local café each Saturday morning to tell their stories and problems. They have created a sense of community and a place women can share their experiences, their goodwill, and their humor.

68 Join a book club or start one of your own by gathering other women who enjoy books, agreeing on a book to read, and then meeting again to discuss the book and how it

relates to your own lives. Cathie told us she has belonged to the same book club since 1965.

Say it with flowers. One group of women 09
assembles for discussion every month, each
one bringing a flower that represents herself
on that day. When all the women are assem-
bled, a beautiful bouquet has been formed,
and it changes from meeting to meeting.

70 Host an international night. Claudette said her group of friends used to have dinners once a month organized around the theme of a particular country, and each guest would have to come dressed in garb associated with that country.

Get on the Internet. Molly uses her online service to connect with her girlfriends. They have developed a newsletter to publish poems and reviews and share ideas. There is a service we have heard about called "Women's Wire," an elec-tronic community where women can log on and talk about their concerns and issues.

A Friendship Ritual

Sue Thoele, author of *The Woman's Book of Courage* and other titles, wanted to formalize her sisterhood with her best friend, Bonnie Hampton, a psychotherapist. As Sue told us, "I really love ritual. I think it touches you at a deep level that is wordless." Bonnie, by her own admission, is "more intellectually than spiritually grounded" and was not sure this ritual business was something she wanted to

do. However, because she valued the friendship, she was willing to try it. They sponta-
neously developed their own ritual, which
focused on their relationship and how their
friendship supported them in their own
lives. These are the ingredients they used,
but you should use whatever has meaning
for you and your friend:

Pink, red, and white rose petals

A statue of a figure that represents their
friendship to them

A list of attributes that each wishes to have
the other friend safeguard in the future

Both women are in their mid-fifties, and each
looks to the other to be an important part of

her life as they grow older. In their ritual, they sat knee to knee, forehead to forehead, and spoke of the items that they had collected. The rose petals stood for patience (pink), passion (red), and purity (white), and as they examined each, they talked of the significance of that emotion or quality in their

present and future lives. As Sue said, "We
are going to get old, and we have always said
that we promise to get old together. In our

ritual, we had very specific requests of each other, and we promised what we would be and do for each other as we age."

Each took something away from the ritual that went beyond words—feelings that only a ceremony can solidify. Sue remembers, "It was wonderful. I am a very security-conscious person. This formalized bond may not change my actions at all, but it adds a different dimension to my life." Bonnie, on the other hand, noted, "I think of myself as a risk taker. Having that ritual allows me to continue to take risks because I know that Sue will take care of me and that she will help my family take care of me in a way that I want. That safe base allows me to take even more risk."

Plan your own ritual with your friend. How you do it and what you use to signify your relationship are not important. Merely taking the time to indicate to each other what you value about each other or to entrust each other with your ultimate goals or worries is significant.  These actions indicate that you recognize the centrality of this relationship to your lives.

Acknowledgments

Many thanks to those who contributed photographs:

Dorothy Bere

Renee Brooks

Carol Coe

Nora Donaghy

Marie-Hélène Fredericks

Ed Grippe

Amy Hall

Julie Herman

Nancy Herman

Beth Hood

Margaret Hood

JuJu Johnson

Dorothy Mann

Tracy McLaughlin

Susan Miller

Dorothy O'Brien

Elizabeth O'Brien

Jeanne Oliver

Donna Scott

Isabelle Selby

Joan Sibley

Leola Specht

Leslie Watkins

Marty Wellington

Leslie Wruble

Phyllis Yelvington

good friends with

woman who wants to

we end up hanging

makes the meanest

could hope for on a

also another medical

who is a mighty att

little party organizer